The Mystery of the Voynich Manuscript

A Captivating Guide to the World's Most Mysterious Book and the Unsolved Code Within

© Copyright 2025 - All rights reserved.

The content contained within this book may not be reproduced, duplicated, or transmitted without direct written permission from the author or the publisher.

Under no circumstances will any blame or legal responsibility be held against the publisher, or author, for any damages, reparation, or monetary loss due to the information contained within this book, either directly or indirectly.

Legal Notice:

This book is copyright protected. It is only for personal use. You cannot amend, distribute, sell, use, quote, or paraphrase any part, or the content within this book, without the consent of the author or publisher.

Disclaimer Notice:

Please note the information contained within this document is for educational and entertainment purposes only. All effort has been executed to present accurate, up-to-date, reliable, and complete information. No warranties of any kind are declared or implied. Readers acknowledge that the author is not engaging in the rendering of legal, financial, medical, or professional advice. The content within this book has been derived from various sources. Please consult a licensed professional before attempting any techniques outlined in this book.

By reading this document, the reader agrees that under no circumstances is the author responsible for any losses, direct or indirect, that are incurred as a result of the use of the information contained within this document, including, but not limited to, errors, omissions, or inaccuracies.

Free Bonus from Captivating History (Available for a Limited time)

Hi History Lovers!

Now you have a chance to join our exclusive history list so you can get your first history ebook for free as well as discounts and a potential to get more history books for free!

Simply visit the link below to join.

Or, Scan the QR code!

captivatinghistory.com/ebook

Also, make sure to follow us on Facebook, X, and YouTube by searching for Captivating History.

Table of Contents

INTRODUCTION: THE MANUSCRIPT THAT BORE HIS NAME 1
CHAPTER 1 - FOLLOWING THE PAPER TRAIL OF THE MANUSCRIPT..........................4
CHAPTER 2 - A CLOSER LOOK AT VOYNICH AND THE MANUSCRIPT.......................11
CHAPTER 3 - TAKING A LOOK INSIDE THE BOOK..................16
CHAPTER 4 - FURTHER ATTEMPTS TO UNRAVEL THE MYSTERY......................21
CHAPTER 5 - THE PHILOSOPHER'S QUEST FOR THE MEANING OF LIFE 27
CHAPTER 6 - A MANUSCRIPT FROM A GALAXY FAR, FAR, AWAY? 31
CONCLUSION - A GREAT ENDURING MYSTERY? OR A GREAT HOAX? 34
HERE'S ANOTHER BOOK BY CAPTIVATING HISTORY THAT YOU MIGHT LIKE.......................37
FREE BONUS FROM CAPTIVATING HISTORY (AVAILABLE FOR A LIMITED TIME) 38
FURTHER READING AND REFERENCES...................39
IMAGE SOURCES 40

Introduction: The Manuscript That Bore His Name

The Voynich Manuscript is one of the most puzzling mysteries ever uncovered. For some, it is easy to cast the manuscript aside as a hoax, but for others, the more they look into this strange saga, the stranger it gets. The manuscript itself consists of several aging pages bound together as one book. It dates back to the Late Middle Ages.

The book is old, but that is not what is so startling about it. After all, there are plenty of old books in the world. It is the contents of the book that stand out as odd. First of all, the book is written in an unknown script. To be clear, this is not a script that has been lost in translation—there are a few of those scattered around the world. Rather, it is a script that has never been seen before.

There is a distinction to be made between these two categories. The ancient language of the Egyptians once fit into the former category; it was a language that had been lost to the ages for many centuries until the Rosetta Stone, found by the armies of Napoleon Bonaparte, finally unlocked the secrets of the once-dead language and translated it for posterity.

There is a big difference between the dead language of an ancient civilization that has since been forgotten and one that had never been heard of at all and of which there are no other known examples. It is almost as if the Voynich Manuscript had been yanked from some unknown realm and dropped here on Earth.

There is no way to translate the words of the manuscript because the words themselves are a complete mystery. Along with the strange words, there are some unusual illustrations that seem to tell their own startling tale. The illustrations feature everything from strange plants to scenes of human beings in baths and vats. These images are interspersed with semi-mechanical piping. This is certainly some odd imagery for a medieval text to have.

Those who dismiss the words as gibberish or a meaningless prank have likely never looked very closely at the Voynich Manuscript. Even though no one knows what the words convey, the book seems to be quite obviously a detailed, technical document of some sort.

The document is believed to be dated from the Late Middle Ages. Most people think it hailed from a period of time known as the Italian Renaissance. This period lasted from the 14th century all the way to the 16th century. It was a time in which many notable creative spirits flourished. Michelangelo, Leonardo da Vinci, and Rafael (the artists—not the Ninja Turtles!) all perfected their craft during this period. The Italian Renaissance was basically the beginning of the more widespread and further-reaching Renaissance that encompassed western Europe.

The Voynich Manuscript would not be discovered by the outside world until a man named Wilfrid Voynich came across the mysterious text in 1912. As you can probably already tell, we get the name for this manuscript from the man who found it.

Wilfrid Voynich was a traveling scholar and a collector of all sorts of strange literary odds and ends. During one of his collecting sprees, Voynich found a treasure box. Inside this cobweb-covered trunk, he laid eyes on a strange, centuries-old manuscript. Little did he know at the time that the manuscript would later bear his name.

It sounds like he was some treasure hunter looking to take things that had been long forgotten. In reality, he did not just take it—he bought it. The monks who were in charge of it were hard-pressed for cash. They were more than willing to part with some old documents for a handsome fee. Voynich would later embellish the story of his finding the manuscript, omitting the simple fact that he paid for it.

It remains unclear why he felt this was necessary, but he apparently thought it just sounded better to say that he snatched it up without paying a dime. It was only after Wilfrid Voynich's passing in 1931 that the truth of how he found the document was revealed by his wife Ethel.

Wilfrid Voynich likely knew that he had stumbled upon a true treasure. He would have been able to deduce this from the strange script he could not read as well as from the script that he could read. There was a letter inside the book written in Latin, which Voynich could read. These Latin words imparted a rather intriguing story surrounding the manuscript.

The letter was marked as having been written on August 19th, 1666. It makes reference to the book as being one of mysterious origins and written in a language that no one can decipher. So, the book being indecipherable is by no means a new phenomenon. People have been having a hard time making heads or tails of it for a long time prior to Voynich's discovery of the manuscript.

The letter contained some further speculation, suggesting that the manuscript had once belonged to Emperor Rudolf II and that it had likely been authored by British scientist and philosopher Roger Bacon. To be sure, these were just theories proposed by someone back in 1666. They did not have any conclusive answers, just as we do not have any today.

Nevertheless, the musings in the letter provided some interesting clues into this strange mystery. This speculative letter piqued Voynich's interest enough to pay the monks money. Voynich was a rather shrewd man, so he likely thought that he would eventually get a return on his investment by promoting the strange manuscript himself.

His efforts would meet with some rather mixed results. He managed to bring the ancient document to the world's attention, but he never really received much of a return on his investment. He ultimately died penniless and deeply in debt. At any rate, his name and the manuscript that bears his name remain quite famous.

Chapter 1 – Following the Paper Trail of the Manuscript

"In 1912, during one of my periodic visits to the Continent of Europe, I came across a most remarkable collection of precious illuminated manuscripts. For many decades these volumes had laid buried in the chest in which I had found them in an ancient castle in Southern Europe. While examining the manuscripts, with a view to the acquisition of at least part of the collection, my attention was especially drawn to one volume. It was such an ugly duckling."

-Wilfrid Voynich[i]

The best way to start unraveling a mystery is to go back to the beginning. As it pertains to the Voynich Manuscript, the furthest back we can go is to the 15th or perhaps the 14th century. The radiocarbon dating results of the Voynich Manuscript tell us that the cattle whose hides provided the material for the pages lived during this time.[ii]

It has been speculated that the actual text must date back somewhere between the early 1300s and the mid-1400s. This was an interesting time period since the Renaissance was taking place. Much was being discovered during this period, but there was still much yet to be known.

---

[i] Kennedy, Gerry. *The Voynich Manuscript: The Mysterious Code That Has Defied Interpretation for Centuries.* 2006. Pg. 14.

[ii] Edwards, H. Robert. *Voynich Reconsidered: The Most Mysterious Manuscript in the World.* 2024. Pg. 1.

During this time, most scholars still believed that the sun and other stars revolved around the earth and that the earth was the center of the universe. The astronomer Galileo Galilei would shatter this illusion forever with his discoveries and theories. Europeans had yet to discover the Americas (at least on a well-known scale; the vast majority of Europeans knew nothing about Leif Eriksson's exploration of North America).

Although there is still some room for debate on this, as far as anyone can tell, those who wrote the text in the Voynich Manuscript likely knew nothing about the vast American continents. This is noteworthy since some of the flora depicted in the manuscript's illustrations resemble some flora native to the Americas. This, of course, only deepens the mystery.

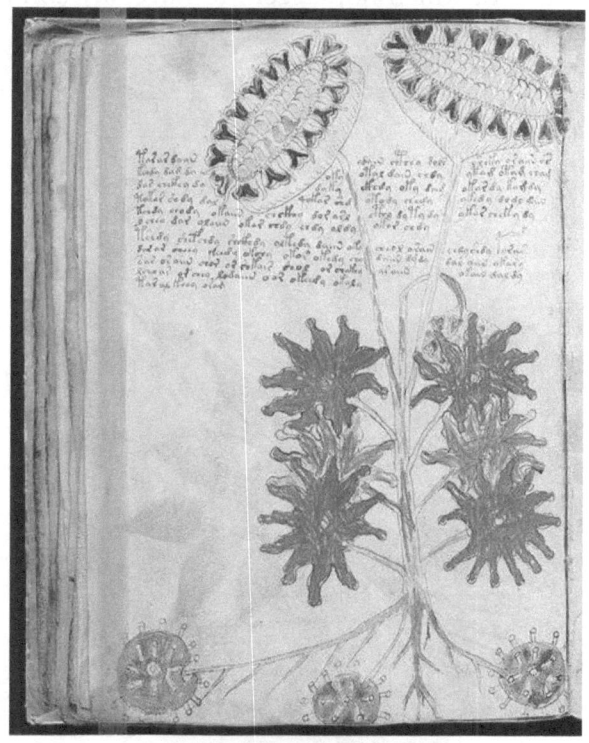

Could this be a sunflower?[1]

It is also important to note that during the period in which the Voynich Manuscript is believed to have been composed, a cultural shift was taking place in Europe as it pertained to bookmaking. Previously, bookmaking had been reserved for monks in remote monasteries.

During the Italian Renaissance, bookmaking was increasingly being transferred to city-based enterprises that focused more on academic and even commercial appeal instead of solely religious consumption.

The actual text is penned in what appears to be dark brown ink, whereas the illustrations are composed largely in blue, green, red, and brown shades of color. Even without being able to translate the text, the drawings themselves seem to tell a stunning story. The illustrations seem to comprise a total of six sections. These sections depict everything from plants, zodiac signs, geometry, strange animals, alchemy, and even naked women.

It is not clear what message the manuscript is trying to convey, but it seems to tell a compelling story. The script is made up of over 100,000 different characters, of which none seem to have any connection to any known language on the planet.

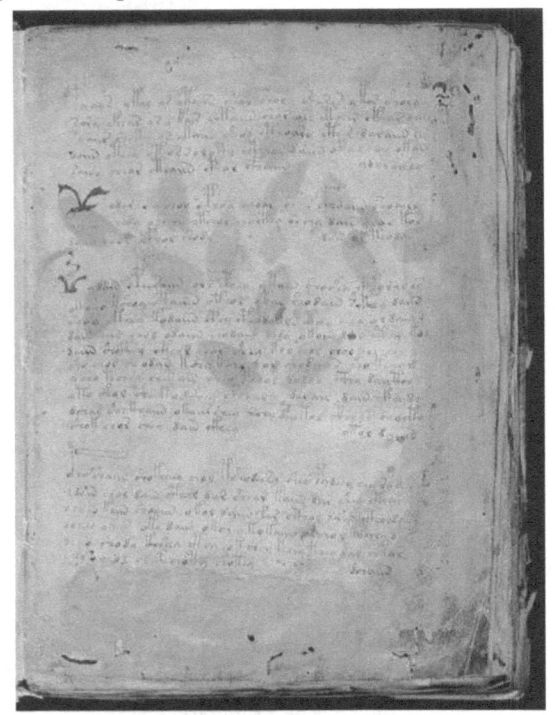

One of the pages of the Voynich Manuscript.[2]

Even so, it is clear by the way the manuscript is arranged that the text is meant to be a readable language of some sort. After the manuscript was compiled, it is believed that it was passed around for a bit and exchanged hands between multiple affluent patrons of the arts. It is unclear if these early owners of the manuscript knew what the words meant either. If they did not understand it (and they most likely did not), then they all purchased it because of the mysterious nature of the text.

It makes one wonder if some medieval huckster slapped the book together as a kind of gimmick just to make a quick buck. Perhaps they went as far as to create a new, made-up language just so they could claim that the text was written in the tongue of angels in order to get rich and curious patrons to shell out their cash to buy it.

It might sound outrageous today to believe that a book was written by angels, but this was a common talking point in medieval circles. One of the most famous medieval scholars who claimed not only to have believed in such things but to actually have deciphered angelic script was a scholar named John Dee. Dee referred to angelic writing as Enochian in reference to the biblical prophet Enoch, who was said to have communed with angels and to have been spirited away by them to the heavens.

We will discuss some of these theories a little more in-depth later in this book, but right now, let us stick to the supposed chain of custody of the Voynich Manuscript. It is widely believed that by the 16th century, the Voynich Manuscript had made its way into the possession of Rudolf II. He reigned supreme over the House of Habsburg and served, for a time, as the Holy Roman emperor.

For those who are not familiar with the history of central Europe, some explanation is in order. The Holy Roman Empire was kickstarted by Charlemagne (the historical ruler, not the rapper). It eventually came to represent a loose confederation of states in mostly central Europe, but at its greatest extent, it also comprised parts of France and Italy. Prior to the existence of Germany, nearly all of the traditional Germanic lands were part of the Holy Roman Empire, and German culture was indeed at its heart.

So, what did Holy Roman Emperor Rudolf II want with the Voynich Manuscript? Well, interestingly enough, he apparently handed the manuscript to a skilled alchemist and druggist by the name of Jacobus Horcicky (or Jacobus Sinapius). This is known because in more recent years, after scanning certain pages of the manuscript with ultraviolet light, this alchemist's long faded signature has been discovered on the very first page of the manuscript. He signed his name as Jacobi a Tepenecz, which was the calling card of a court physician named Jacobus Horcicky.

He was a skilled physician and had been credited with healing the emperor of a terrible ailment. In fact, this feat granted him the noble title of "a Tepenecz," which is in reference to Tepenec Castle.

So, it would seem that the emperor's personal doctor was looking very closely at the text of the Voynich Manuscript. What was he looking for? And did he discover anything? It is worth noting that since Horcicky had experience working with chemistry and herbal medicines, he likely found the section of the manuscript seemingly devoted to strange and exotic plants, herbs, and alchemy rather intriguing.

The fact that such an esteemed scholar took the book so seriously seems to indicate that neither Rudolf II nor the good doctor felt that the manuscript was a hoax. To them, it was something real, impressive, and immeasurably valuable.

Horcicky passed away in 1622. Another reference to the manuscript was made over a decade later, in 1637, by way of a note penned in Latin. The letter was written by Georg Baresch, a Bohemian scholar and alchemist. He was not a doctor of medicine like Horcicky, but he was also apparently researching the strange and mysterious words of the Voynich Manuscript.

Georg Baresch likely sent a copy of some of the characters from the Voynich manuscript to Athanasius Kircher, a Jesuit priest. Kircher had created a Coptic dictionary and was thought to have discovered the meaning of Egyptian hieroglyphics. These letters were exchanged, of course, prior to the days of copy machines, faxes, scanners, email attachments, and the like, so the only way for a "copy" of a document to be sent from one scholar to another was by copying it by hand!

Baresch did not receive a reply from Kircher, so he reached out again. The follow-up letter that Georg Baresch sent is the one that has been preserved for posterity. This letter—also written in Latin—spoke of a perplexing manuscript with strange, unknown characters that no one had been able to figure out. Baresch expressed his hopes that Kircher might be able to unravel the mystery of the strange text.

Georg Baresch mentions the illustrations that have long captured the imaginations of so many. He speaks of how there are illustrations of plants, herbs, stars, and many other things, which he viewed as being somehow related to holistic healing and medicine. He also mentioned that many of the exotic plants were not anything ever seen before in his particular part of Europe.

Kircher eventually replied and also took note of the strange nature of the manuscript and its undecipherable characters. He wanted to try to figure out what the strange text might mean (if anything). He ended his letter by suggesting that he would do his best to try and unravel the mystery whenever he had time to do so.

However, this man, just like so many others, would ultimately perish before learning how to decipher even one word of the text. What strikes one as strange, perhaps, is the fact that Kircher seemed confident that he would be able to decipher the manuscript at all. Most linguists today take a much more dismal view of their prospects.

So, why was Kircher so sure of himself? Was this some sort of false bravado just to make himself look more competent than he actually was, especially since he was trying to impress a potential benefactor? It certainly would not be the first time (or the last time) that such things had happened. Or were scholars like Kirchner, who were much closer to the source and origin point of the manuscript, more confident in deciphering it because they knew something that we do not? Perhaps they knew something that we have since lost?

Kirchner seemed to think that the language was somehow related to the Illyrian language of the ancient Indo-European-speaking peoples of the Balkans. Could Kirchner have been on to something after all?

Georg Baresch passed away around the year of 1662. We know this because in a letter penned in 1662, one of his colleagues, Johannes Marcus Marci, penned a letter that spoke of Georg Baresch's death and how he had inherited much of the collections of his personal library.

As far as the Voynich Manuscript is concerned, it does seem that the strange text was a part of the library that Marci inherited. Marci was a Czech scientist, physician, and scholar who worked at Charles University in Prague.

Marci began to open up the dialogue with Kircher about the text. On August 19th, 1665, Marci fired off a note to Kircher in which he spoke about his belief that Kircher would be able to finally unlock the meaning of the text and read what the strange characters conveyed.

One of the more interesting things about this letter was Marci's personal conviction that the original manuscript might have been penned by the British alchemist Sir Roger Bacon. If such a thing were true, that would mean the manuscript is older than what radiocarbon dating has suggested. Roger Bacon died in the year 1292. Even if he penned the manuscript during his last year of life, that puts the age of the manuscript as being older than the previous estimates, which placed its creation in the first few decades of the 1300s at the very latest.

Whatever the case may be, there does not seem to have been a response to Marci's inquiry into the origin of the manuscript. The letter was received, but it sat unanswered for centuries, ultimately getting stuffed inside the mysterious manuscript itself. It was not until Wilfrid Voynich stumbled upon the manuscript and this corresponding letter in the early 20th century that such things were brought to light again.

Chapter 2 – A Closer Look at Voynich and the Manuscript

"The files [of the Irkutsk region] preserved the track record of M. Voynich's pharmaceutical activities, compiled by the Warsaw Medical Council in 1886, from which it is clear that Voynich often moved from one city to another (Kovno, Minsk, Vilno, Warsaw). It was in these large cities that the Proletariat party concentrated its activities, on whose instructions Voynich carried out."

-Vladimir Pavlovich Skorokhodov, Russian historian[i]

On April 20th, 1921, Wilfrid Voynich delivered a document to the College of Physicians of Philadelphia. The document seems to indicate that he was writing to people who had a rather large amount of cash at their disposal. The document was headed with the name of "A Preliminary Sketch of the History of the Roger Bacon Cipher Manuscript."

The heading seems to indicate Voynich's preoccupation with the concept that Roger Bacon was indeed the original author of the manuscript. He insisted that Bacon seemed the most likely author because of his own belief that the manuscript dated back to Bacon's time.

---

[i] Edwards, H. Robert. *Voynich Reconsidered: The Most Mysterious Manuscript in the World.* 2024. Pg. 11.

Roger Bacon had been persecuted for some of his scientific findings, which his enemies had misconstrued as attempts to engage in wizardry and witchcraft. Voynich theorized that this was the reason for his secrecy and why he might write an encyclopedic work like the Voynich Manuscript.

Even though Roger Bacon did not delve into witchcraft, Wilfrid Voynich felt Bacon believed it was necessary to mask his legitimate scientific research in code, lest his opponents try to misrepresent his work. It does make sense that Bacon would have wanted to reveal his findings when they were complete. If that was the case, he would have kept a key to unlock his carefully crafted code.

Wilfrid Voynich left those who listened to him absolutely riveted by his interpretation of events. They ate up his story, and they loved what they heard. But, of course, the radiocarbon dating, which was done at a later date, has since dispelled the notion that Roger Bacon could have been the author of this strange and mysterious document.

A photograph of Wilfrid Voynich.[8]

Wilfrid Voynich was quite a character. In our exploration of the mysteries of the Voynich Manuscript, it would be worth our while to take note of the life and many eccentricities of Wilfrid Voynich (born Michał Habdank-Wojnicz).

The man who discovered (or re-discovered) the manuscript that would henceforth bear his name was born on October 31st (Halloween, no less), 1864. The son of a Polish barrister, Wilfrid Voynich was born in a land that was part of the Russian Empire. He was born in the town of Telšiai in the Russian province of Kovno in a region that is now part of the independent state of Lithuania.

Not a whole lot is known about Voynich's early years. It is believed that he was a Pole by ethnicity and that he likely spoke Polish as a native language, although he would acquire many languages during his life.

Of course, Russian would have been a language that Voynich would have known well, and he apparently used it with ease. However, he was not always able to talk himself out of trouble when he became entangled with the Russian authorities. Nevertheless, on November 27th, 1884, Voynich managed to graduate from the University of Moscow at the age of twenty with a degree as a pharmaceutical chemist.

Voynich's other activities gained him the ire of the Russian authorities. In these pre-revolutionary days, the imperial Russian Crown was desperately trying to maintain its grip on power. Voynich became involved with some more radical circles of Russian thinkers.

On October 10th, 1885, he gained notice from the Russian authorities for his involvement with a radical group dubbed the International Social Revolutionary Party, or as they were better known, the Proletariat. The Russian tsar viewed such movements as a direct threat to his rule and sought to crack down on them at all costs.

Wilfrid Voynich fell prey to this crackdown, and as with many others in this sweep, he was arrested. On April 30th, 1887, he was summarily sentenced without so much as a trial to five years of hard labor in the cold wastelands of Siberia. It was a fate that many Russians faced under the tsar of imperialist Russia, as well as under the later dictatorships of communist Russia. Voynich ended up staying in the harsh frontier city of Irkutsk. Then, on December 7th, 1887, he was transferred to the small town of Tunka, which bordered Mongolia. Tunka was apparently even worse than Irkutsk because Voynich was soon petitioning the governor general of Irkutsk to be able to return.

On June 21st, 1889, he was granted that permission. Voynich stayed in Irkutsk for another year, but after a series of complaints about his health, he requested to be moved to Balagansk, which he felt had a better climate. Around a year later, on June 12th, 1890, he was allowed to make this move.

But the thing is, Voynich never arrived at Balagansk. Instead, we have a police record from July 6th, 1890, that states he officially went missing. Was Voynich simply lost in the shuffle, or did he plan for a jailbreak all along? Whatever the case was, the manhunt that followed would carry on for several weeks.

It was no use, though, since Voynich was already on his way to Britain. How did he get there? Well, it was a daring escape. It seems that Voynich must have traveled by train from Siberia to Germany and then went to France before he took a boat across the English Channel to Britain. It is known that he arrived in the city of London on October 5th, 1890. He was twenty-six years old at the time.

What exactly transpired once he arrived in the capital of England is not exactly clear and remains largely shrouded in mystery. Some have suggested that he was able to hook up with other Russian revolutionaries, which seems to indicate that his escape was part of a larger plan.

At any rate, he eventually met a woman named Ethel Lilian Boole, a British writer and the daughter of the famous mathematician George Boole (who developed Boolean algebra). Voynich would eventually marry Ethel.

The next official record of Voynich comes to us from Britain's 1901 census. In this census, Voynich was listed as living with Ethel Lilian Boole, and his occupation was categorized as "bookseller and bibliographer." This was a fitting title for the discoverer of the ancient Voynich Manuscript. Voynich gave his place of birth as "Russian Poland."

He married Ethel Boole the following year, with the two of them getting hitched in 1902. Voynich's age upon his marriage was listed as being thirty-eight years of age. Voynich then became a naturalized citizen of Britain on April 25th, 1904. A few years later, in 1912, Voynich discovered the manuscript that would later make him so famous.

A couple of years after this discovery, in 1914, Voynich first ventured across the Atlantic to the United States. It was apparently during this trip that he embarked upon his first known efforts to sell the Voynich

Manuscript. Can we blame him? Voynich needed to pay the bills after all! But no matter how much he tried to sell the ancient manuscript, he could not. Voynich found it exceedingly hard to find a buyer.

Ultimately, he would die with the manuscript still in his possession. He perished on March 19th, 1930, from lung cancer. He had succeeded in neither selling nor unraveling the mystery of the Voynich manuscript. It was not until after Voynich was dead that it was purchased by a book dealer named Hans Peter Kraus. Kraus donated it to Yale University, where it remains to this very day.

Chapter 3 – Taking a Look Inside the Book

"Cipher manuscript on vellum. Text written in a secret script, apparently based on Roman miniscule characters, irregularly disposed on pages. 102 leaves (of 116; lacks 14 leaves), including 7 double folio folding leaves; 3 triple folio folding leaves; and one quadruple folding leaf. With added signature marks. With about 400 drawings of botanical subjects, including many of full-page size; 33 drawings of astrological or astronomical subjects, plus about 350 single star-figures; and 42 (biological?) drawings."

-Hans Peter Kraus[i]

So far, we have highlighted much of the background and supposed origins of the Voynich Manuscript. But what about the book itself? What about the mysterious contents inside the book? At a glance, the book is not very impressive. You may be picturing it as some great, huge grimoire-styled tome, but it is actually as big as a run-of-the-mill paperback.

The book consists of around 240 pages in total, although this does depend on what one might quantify as being a page. The pages were once numbered, with numerals scrawled into the upper right corner. This was apparently done many years after the manuscript was first

---

[i] Edwards, H. Robert. *Voynich Reconsidered: The Most Mysterious Manuscript in the World.* 2024. Pgs. 21-22.

composed, but according to this numerical count, the pages only number 116.

How could there be such a discrepancy in page count? It is due to all of the fold-out pages and whether or not they are counted in the number. There are pages within this manuscript known as folios with page leaves that fold out so that mural-like illustrations can be better depicted. However, it is worth noting that it is widely believed that eight potential pages are missing from the manuscript.[i]

This can only make one wonder (or hope) that if those missing pages ever turn up, they will hold the key to deciphering the whole manuscript. Would it not be interesting if one of those missing pages actually had its own version of the Rosetta Stone? With a known language such as English, French, or German directly translated into the unknown language of the manuscript, we could finally understand what was actually written in the text.

Much of the Voynich Manuscript's illustrations depict plant life. However, much of the plant life (at least in the manner presented in the manuscript) is not known to exist in the real world. During the medieval period, it was noted that such things did not exist in central Europe, and as far as anyone can tell, they do not exist anywhere else on Earth.

Some of the illustrations are clearly fanciful in scope, such as a depiction of a plant growing out of the body of a cat. There is also a depiction of a plant that seems to have faces secured to the roots. Unless there is some alien world out there that hosts such bizarre manifestations, these drawings come from the fanciful imagination of its illustrator.

Around 129 pages (counting all of the folios) of the manuscript are part of the so-called "herbal section." As mentioned earlier, the illustrations are in color, with green, red, blue, and brown seeming to be the primary colors used to illustrate them. It is not exactly the most striking arrangement, but the illustrations stand out all the same.

Many of the drawings depict leaf-bearing plants, flowers, berries, and roots. These are parts of plants that would be useful for herbal concoctions.

---

[i] Belfield, Richard. *The Six Unsolved Ciphers: Inside the Mysterious Codes That Have Confounded the World's Greatest Cryptographers.* 2007. Pg. 83.

A page from the Voynich Manuscript.'

This is all well and good for the plant section, but what about the astronomical section? There is a section of folios that appear to depict stars, planets, the sun, and the like. These depictions seem to have an astronomical and astrological theme.

The concept of astrology, of course, is an ancient one, and it contends that the position and movements of celestial bodies somehow have an influence on the lives of humans. The section that includes astrological charts contains most, but curiously, not all of the zodiac constellations.

But even more perplexing than what may be written in the stars is the "biological" or "balneological" section of the book. This section seems to depict several illustrations of nude female human beings immersed in containers full of some sort of liquid. These containment units are connected to each other with what looks like some sort of piping.

Even though the manuscript is from over five hundred years ago, these pages seem as if they are taken from some sort of disturbing science fiction narrative. One could easily let their imagination run away with these depictions. Some people even openly speculate that the illustrations are depicting cloning or some sort of confinement by an alien life force. The women, for the most part at least, do not seem to be under duress; they are depicted as just sitting or standing in quiet repose while immersed in water (or whatever liquid it might be).

Along with these very strange illustrations are the characters and glyphs that seem to serve as captions. What stories they could tell if we could only read them! Even though we do not yet understand what message (if any) they might convey, the text seems to follow some very clear patterns. These patterns form linguistic strings of information that are just crying out for someone out there to unlock their meaning.

In all of the years of studying this enigmatic text, one thing seems to have been learned with a fair amount of certainty. The writing found within the manuscript is entirely unique, whether it is a hoax or just an extremely rare example of a lost language. There does not appear to be any other written script on the planet that can be said to match the writing found in the Voynich Manuscript.

If the text is a hoax, it is a hoax done well. As many who have studied the manuscript have noted, there does not seem to be the slightest hint of uncertainty from whoever penned the text. The text seems to have been written down with confidence and self-assurance. If someone was making it up as they went along, the bold, clear, and solid brushstrokes of the pen do not seem to indicate such. If it was all made up, one may expect some uncertainty in the lines, even perhaps some errors and mistakes. But everything seems to flow freely and perfectly.

Even though the language of the text is not understood, there is a clear consensus that the text is written from left to right and is most likely read from left to right as well. This is, of course, in line with most scripts that have their origins in the Western world. English, German, French, Italian, and other languages are all written and read from left to right.

One has to go to India, China, and Japan to find scripts that are read from the opposite direction.

Another thing that has been noted is that the text and the glyphs are made up of several lines of horizontal text and that many more are "left justified." This leads most scholars to assume that the text of the Voynich Manuscript is either related to or, at the very least, inspired by known European languages. This is interesting, considering the fact that recent attempts to crack the code by utilizing AI (artificial intelligence) tools have led to a different conclusion. AI has consistently noted a relationship between the text and the Middle Eastern language of Hebrew, not European languages.

One thing that stands out about the written script of the Voynich Manuscript is the fact there is no punctuation present in the sentences. There are no commas, periods, colons, semi-colons, or any other clear form of stop punctuation. Instead of utilizing any of these literary speed bumps, the script is free-flowing like a river.

Although there is no definitive proof of there being any connection, it has long been said that the characters have a general resemblance to the ancient Persian Pahlavi script. This in itself is fairly interesting since the Persian script is written right to left rather than from left to right.

The written script, in many ways, is an anomaly. Every aspect of it stands out. As it pertains to the manuscript as a whole, Wilfrid Voynich himself once dubbed it an "ugly duckling" of a book.[i] And this odd uniqueness can be seen throughout the entirety of the text.

---

[i] Voynich, Wilfrid. *A Preliminary Sketch of the History of the Roger Bacon Manuscript.* 1921.

Chapter 4 – Further Attempts to Unravel the Mystery

"Toying with the Voynich Manuscript is like playing a pinball machine. Start the ball rolling and it will hit and light up images at every turn of its trajectory until it disappears down a dark sump below."

-Gerry Kennedy[1]

The closer one looks at the Voynich Manuscript, the stranger it seems to be. In fact, some of the drawings appear to capture something so small and delicate as to be microscopic.

It has long been asserted that whoever drew the illustrations of the plant life must have had some sort of advanced knowledge of plant structure and perhaps even access to a primitive microscope. The first real microscope was not invented until the late 16th century. Since the Voynich Manuscript predates this discovery by a couple of hundred years, it remains a mystery how the illustrator managed to capture such fine detail, which could seemingly only be known by looking at a plant at the microscopic level.

Considering the fact that it was long believed by many who handled the document—even Voynich himself—that the great English scholar Roger Bacon was the one who penned it, such things seem rather telling. Could it be that Roger Bacon, who is today hailed as a genius, was much

---

[1] Kennedy, Gerry. *The Voynich Manuscript: The Mysterious Code That Has Defied Interpretation for Centuries.* 2006. Pg. 26.

smarter than anyone ever realized? Was he really so smart that he understood and delved into the microscopic world hundreds of years before anyone else? And if so, why would he have kept it secret?

Well, as it turns out, being cautious and secretive in regard to scientific discoveries was a wise approach back in those days. The threat of retribution from Catholic Church officials over any new findings that were deemed to be heretical was just too great. As such, brilliant minds such as Roger Bacon were wise to be cautious in how they documented their findings and when (if ever) they revealed what they had discovered to the rest of the world.

Bacon was a rather interesting man. He had developed a complex scientific approach that defied most of the church teachings of his day, yet he himself never lost his own faith in God. Prior to Christopher Columbus sailing the ocean blue, some theologians were still convinced the earth was flat. Roger Bacon was one of the few who knew better, but he was not about to boast in public of his theories and findings. He kept those things in private confidence.

It seems that one event in particular made Bacon even more private. In 1268, Bacon's best benefactor, Pope Clement IV, perished in 1268. Bacon knew that enemies of the deceased pope might be on the lookout for a way to strike at the pope's formerly loyal custodians of knowledge, such as himself. Many agree that Bacon likely had both the ability and the motivation to encrypt his most secret writings in an unbreakable cipher, such as what might be presented in the Voynich Manuscript.

But if it was Bacon's book, then what is it all about? Is it merely a scientific breakthrough of his day, such as the discovery of microscopic organisms? But what about the "biological" section of the manuscript? How might this be related?

The folios that make up the so-called "biological" or "balneological" section of the Voynich Manuscript are perhaps the second-most prominent section after the plant section. It is one of the most startling since it prominently features nude women inside strange contraptions, which look like baths or vats connected to some sort of biological or mechanical piping.

Weird is the best word to describe these illustrations. But what is interesting is that some researchers believe this section of the book focuses on women's health, perhaps aspects of women's health that were taboo at the time the book was created.

It has been suggested that this section might be a guide on women's sexual health, covering everything from sexual practices to herbal contraceptives to even herbal abortion techniques. In some ways, it is almost hard to argue against this theory, as the odd imagery seems to show women (some of whom look pregnant) in odd poses bathing in herbal solutions.

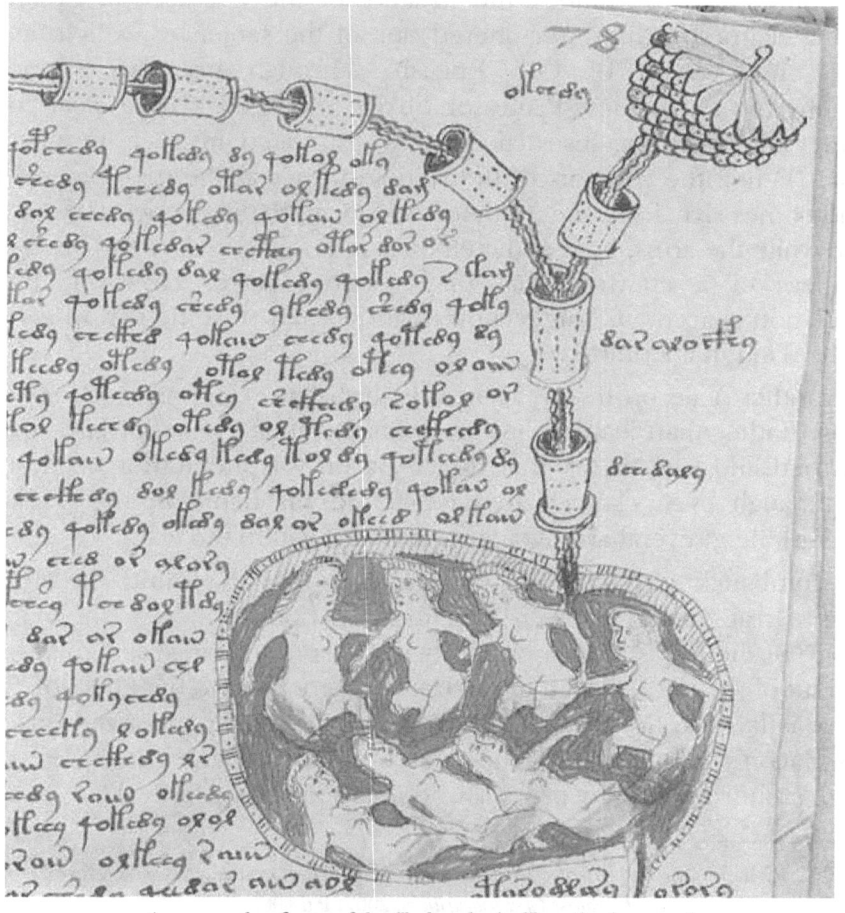

An example of one of the "balneological" section's pages.[5]

One person who championed this theory was a professor from Yale University, where the manuscript ended up, Professor Leonell Strong. Strong was well established in the medical field and used his expertise in medicine and cryptography to come up with his own method for cracking the code. In particular, he made use of what he described as being certain arithmetical progressions of the alphabetical letters, which he could supposedly track throughout the text. Somehow or other, this led the professor to believe that the manuscript's true author was an herbalist by the name of Anthony Askham.[i]

Askham was certainly capable enough to author the text since he had a great knowledge of not only herbs but also math, astronomy, and languages. Askham was also known for his almanacs and herbal guides.

In his efforts to unlock the mystery of the manuscript, Professor Strong claimed to have deciphered one of the sentences, which he felt was some variant of Old English. Through his own supposed deciphering techniques, Professor Strong rendered what appear to be some rather startling instructions. The translated instructions possibly read, "When the contents of the veins rip (or tear the membranes) the child comes slyly from the mother issuing with the leg-stance skewed and bent while the arms, bent at the elbow, are knotted (above the head) like the legs of a crawfish."[ii] That may sound strange. However, if the translation is accurate, this section might be part of some sort of general guide to aid in childbirth.

Another Yale professor, Robert Brumbaugh, came up with his own ideas. Rather than leaning on the Askham theory, he went back to the old tried and true theory that Roger Bacon was the author of the text. Brumbaugh even claimed to have found his name in the book by unscrambling several arrangements of letters within the text.[iii]

Brumbaugh also claimed that he had actually found the key to decipher the manuscript near the end of the book written on the margins of one of the folios.[iv] He supposedly uncovered a strange statement near the end of the book, which he said stated something to the effect of "The above is false so do not take it." Brumbaugh actually theorized that this was Bacon's admission that he was committing fraud just to get some quick cash from wealthy patrons who might purchase his text.[v]

---

[i] Belfield, Richard. *The Six Unsolved Ciphers: Inside the Mysterious Codes That Have Confounded the World's Greatest Cryptographers.* 2007. Pg. 106.

[ii] Belfield, Richard. *The Six Unsolved Ciphers: Inside the Mysterious Codes That Have Confounded the World's Greatest Cryptographers.* 2007. Pg. 107.

[iii] Belfield, Richard. *The Six Unsolved Ciphers: Inside the Mysterious Codes That Have Confounded the World's Greatest Cryptographers.* 2007. Pg. 107.

[iv] Belfield, Richard. *The Six Unsolved Ciphers: Inside the Mysterious Codes That Have Confounded the World's Greatest Cryptographers.* 2007. Pg. 107.

[v] Belfield, Richard. *The Six Unsolved Ciphers: Inside the Mysterious Codes That Have Confounded the World's Greatest Cryptographers.* 2007. Pg. 107.

So, we somehow find ourselves back at the beginning with a small twist. Could it be that Roger Bacon is the author as well as a medieval fraudster? Such things are perhaps a bit insulting to Bacon's legacy, but there is much about this manuscript that remains unknown.

Brumbaugh's investigative efforts led him to conclude that the script might have been an early attempt to create an artificial language based on the lingua franca of old—Latin. Latin was the language of the Roman Empire and the basic template upon which European languages based their script. Long after the Roman Empire had fallen, official court documents, medical journals, and scientific theories were commonly written in Latin. It was basically a universal language that the great thinkers of Europe—whether their native tongue was French, German, English, or the like—could easily understand.

However, by Roger Bacon's day, Latin was falling out of fashion since other European languages had become more prominent. During this transitional period, some great minds like Bacon tinkered with the idea of creating a brand-new universal language that could be used between the nation-states of Europe. Therefore, it has been theorized that the script found in the Voynich Manuscript could have been such an attempt and that it used Latin as its template.[i] This could very well be the case, or it could very well be that the original script was simply Latin that had been thoroughly encrypted.

This particular theory has been put forward by many others. One researcher, a University of Pennsylvania professor by the name of William Newbold, thought that by simply rearranging some letters, he had cracked the code. At one point, he was able to take a seemingly random gibberish-filled sentence, "michiton oladabas multos te tcr cerc portas," and rearrange it into the Latin phrase of "michi dabas multas portas."

"Portas" might have led this particular researcher to think this since *portas* is Latin for "portal" or "gate." Newbold translated the sentence to read, "To me, thou gavest many portals."[ii]

---

[i] Belfield, Richard. *The Six Unsolved Ciphers: Inside the Mysterious Codes That Have Confounded the World's Greatest Cryptographers.* 2007. Pg. 110.

[ii] Belfield, Richard. *The Six Unsolved Ciphers: Inside the Mysterious Codes That Have Confounded the World's Greatest Cryptographers.* 2007. Pgs. 102-103.

Maybe it is saying many portals to many secrets? There could be many secrets yet to be uncovered if and when the strange text of the Voynich Manuscript is completely deciphered. There are those who think that the Voynich Manuscript might even offer up the greatest secret of all—the meaning of life itself.

Chapter 5 – The Philosopher's Quest for the Meaning of Life

"I spent about two and a half years using triads based on the position of the letters, disregarding word spaces and, of course, looking for Latin. The method seemed to have its ups and downs; for months I constantly felt a day away from the solution. I finally threw all my work sheets out and stayed away from the manuscript for six months."

-Leo Levitov[1]

Some would have you believe that the Voynich Manuscript is just another attempt to unravel the greatest mystery of all: the meaning behind our very existence. For those who have tried to find a solid reason behind our existence, this quest often proves to be a fairly disappointing one. We all have finite lives that can seem quite meaningless, all things considered. Finding specific reasons for our existence, for some solid, soul-defining meaning of life, is a hard-won quest.

And for anyone who thinks too deeply about the seeming meaninglessness of our blip of a life in the grand scheme of things, it can be downright discouraging. The average human is incredibly lucky if they live to be one hundred years old. Yet, even this rare soul has only lived for a small fraction of one thousand years. Humans are believed to have

---

[1] Levitov, Leo. *Solution of the Voynich Manuscript: A Liturgical Manual for the Endura Rite of the Cathari Heresy, The Cult of Isis.* 1987. Pg. 4.

been in existence—at least as we know it thus far—for millions of years. The earth is estimated to be over four billion years old. The universe of which the earth is a part is believed to be around fourteen billion years old.

Pretty depressing, right? Yet, throughout the ages, many have carried on this quest to find greater meaning. Could it be that someone came closer to understanding the big questions of the universe than others? Could it be that some of the proposed answers to these questions are locked inside the coded phrases of the Voynich Manuscript?

Of course, one man's meaning of life could very well be what another man considers heresy. According to the work and research of a scholar named Leo Levitov, it could very well be a case of both. Levitov came to the conclusion that the manuscript was likely a holdover from the medieval religious sect known as the Cathars.

The Cathars were a fringe group of Christians with beliefs deemed to be heretical. Most of their beliefs had been inherited by the Christian Gnostics who had come before them. The Gnostics were an early sect of Christianity that had become popular around the 2nd century. This group insisted that there was much more knowledge—secret, hidden knowledge—to be gleaned from the teachings of Christ about the very nature of reality. The term Gnostic, after all, is derived from *gnosis*—the Greek word for knowledge.

The Gnostics were a group of deep thinkers who sought to unify some Christian beliefs that seemed to be at odds. For example, for many early Christians, the tone of the Old Testament, which spoke of the often angry and even vengeful God Jehovah, compared to the message of peace, love, and forgiveness of Jesus Christ in the New Testament was hard to square. To put it quite simply, for many early Christians, the God of the Old Testament seemed mean while Jesus seemed nice. They questioned this and sought answers for this perceived shift in temperament. For the Gnostics, the solution was to proclaim that the creator God, Jehovah or Yahweh, was evil and had wrongly usurped the role of the true God represented by Jesus Christ.

Gnostic beliefs flourished during the 2nd century. For a time, the Gnostic branch of Christianity was a strong rival to orthodox Christian beliefs. It was only after Roman Emperor Constantine made Christianity the official religion of the Roman Empire and set down the official prescribed doctrine at the Council of Nicaea in 325 CE that the Gnostics were firmly placed into the heretical camp. Those who practiced the Gnostic variant of Christianity were suppressed.

However, this suppression was not entirely successful, as was evidenced in the 13th century when the Cathar sect, which embraced a variant of Gnostic beliefs, rose up in western Europe. In order to snuff this Gnostic revival out, the pope actually sanctioned a Crusade to root the Cathars out of France and their other European strongholds. People were killed, and books were burned.

Voynich researcher Leo Levitov's theory is that the Voynich Manuscript is one of the rare surviving texts that had been encrypted by the Cathars.[i] Considering the Crusade and subsequent inquisitions wiped most of the Cathars out and made sure that any survivors toed the Catholic line, the fact that any surviving text would be encrypted in a code would not be surprising.

Leo Levitov suggests that the Cathars essentially hid their own interpretation of the meaning of life. Levitov insists that the book is likely part of their liturgy, which expresses their Gnostic worldview. The main and most important view of the Gnostics was that they believed that all physical material was irrevocably evil. They believed that the material universe was created by the evil Jehovah of the Old Testament and that the divine sparks of the spirit of which humanity is a part have been trapped in this lower material form. This was the Cathars' explanation of who we are and where we (as in humanity) came from.

They furthermore believed that it was the end goal of Christianity to be freed from our physical bodies and have our divine essence leave the physical universe entirely by rising to a higher plane where the true originator of all things—the true God—resides. They believed that Jesus was the divine soul who plunged down into the murky depths of the physical universe to help pull the rest of us out.

Such notions likely resonated with those who were disgusted with their everyday lives in the often cruel and harsh world in which they lived. The only problem was that such ideas were (and still are) completely at odds with what mainline Christianity taught. Those who propagated these beliefs realized the need for secrecy and, therefore, made sure to cover their tracks as much as they could. What better way

---

[i] Levitov, Leo. *Solution of the Voynich Manuscript: A Liturgical Manual for the Endura Rite of the Cathari Heresy, The Cult of Isis.* 1987. Pg. 7.

to do that than to encrypt their beliefs in a manuscript?

According to Leo Levitov, such a connection would also explain the biological section with its emphasis on women. Gnosticism was popular with and heavily influenced by women, who played a prominent role in the sect. One of the chief criticisms of the Cathars, besides their worldview and attempts to explain the meaning of life, was their push toward women's liberation. They even had a bent toward free love in which the bounds of traditional and monogamous relationships championed by mainline Christians were cast to the side.[i]

If this were indeed the case and the manuscript really was a surviving remnant of the Cathars, then the question must be asked: how did it survive? Was the inquisition just not thorough enough? It stands to reason that one or two manuscripts might have slipped through even the most dogged of persecutions.

Also, if Levitov's theory about the Voynich Manuscript is correct, one cannot help but note the irony that the Catholic Church, which snuffed out the Cathars, would end up safeguarding one of their encoded manuscripts. After all, the Voynich Manuscript ended up in the possession of Jesuits who lived in a monastery before falling into the hands of Wilfrid Voynich.

As interesting as the Cathar theory is, it seems that we are once again left with more questions than answers.

---

[i] Levitov, Leo. *Solution of the Voynich Manuscript: A Liturgical Manual for the Endura Rite of the Cathari Heresy, The Cult of Isis.* 1987. Pg. 11.

Chapter 6 – A Manuscript from a Galaxy Far, Far, Away?

One of the more interesting things about the Voynich Manuscript is its alienness, for lack of a better term. This alienness does not present itself to the casual viewer immediately but rather gradually. Its strange, unusual, out-of-place nature has struck many experienced historical researchers as profoundly odd.

Botanists, for example, have spent many long hours studying the plants depicted in the manuscript and have come away from the experience entirely perplexed as to what they had actually been looking at. On the surface, some initially noted some similarities to known plant life, but a deeper investigation only left them with the strange notion that these plants were somehow not of this Earth (or at least any Earth they knew).

This feeling of utter alienness when contemplating the mysteries of the Voynich Manuscript was seconded by astronomers who tried to take a crack at the astronomy and astrology sections of the manuscript. They took a peek at what initially seemed like familiar constellations and began to identify known celestial landmarks, such as the Andromeda Nebula, Hyades, and Aldebaran, only to suddenly get that same strange feeling that something was just not right. It is as if someone looked up at the Big Dipper, enjoying the night sky, only to realize that one or two stars were decidedly out of place.

It is an eerie feeling that seems to defy all explanation. If we are not careful, such things can make one go down the rabbit hole and come up with all manner of bizarre conspiracy theories, ranging from the manuscript being left by extraterrestrials to it being an artifact from an alternate universe that somehow got transported to medieval Europe.

Before we open our minds so broadly, we would be wise to factor in the potential for creative license on the part of the manuscript's composers. All of these strange variations could simply be artistic flourishes by those who were behind the manuscript's illustrations.

The imagery of the zodiac signs arranged among the stars is certainly interesting. One of the more shocking observations is that one of the images of a spiral constellation looks like a depiction of our own Milky Way galaxy. No one has ever taken a photo of our galaxy since humans have yet to venture outside of it, so all that we really have are illustrations. And the illustration in the Voynich Manuscript, at least for some, bears an uncanny resemblance to what we believe the Milky Way would look like from the outside. Not only that, our best ideas of the depiction of the Milky Way seem to form a match when superimposed on the drawing.

They match except for one odd difference—the Voynich Manuscript's depiction of the Milky Way seems to be from a vantage point far outside of the galaxy.[1] Our current depictions of our home galaxy are created looking head-on at the rim of the galaxy, which, on a clear night, is visible in the night sky from our vantage point on Earth. The spiral illustration in the Voynich Manuscript—if it is indeed a depiction of the Milky Way—seems to show how it would look from outside the galaxy at a distance, as if it were drawn by someone who had firsthand knowledge of what approaching the galaxy from afar might look like.

As strange as this sounds and as quick as we might be to dismiss it outright, it gets even weirder. This outside view of the galaxy essentially comes equipped with a "you are here" legend on its galactic map. Bizarrely enough, there is a noticeable blue dot in this diagram, and it is located at the edge of one of the spiral arms, right where we believe the Earth is located in the Milky Way galaxy.

---

[1] Kennedy, Gerry. *The Voynich Manuscript: The Mysterious Code That Has Defied Interpretation for Centuries.* 2006. Pg. 28.

Some claim that the blue dot is just a smudge of ink inadvertently placed on the manuscript. And it could be as simple as that. It is quite likely that people's minds have had tricks played on them because of a mere ink smudge and that the spiral design in the manuscript is nothing more than a random abstract design. But then again, what if it is not? Could this manuscript have been made by someone with a startling knowledge of the cosmos and our place in it? We can only wonder.

Conclusion – A Great Enduring Mystery? Or a Great Hoax?

After hundreds of years of attempting to decipher the Voynich Manuscript, no attempt has been successful. One must then consider the possibility that the reason why the riddle cannot be solved is that there was no riddle to begin with. Could it be that the Voynich Manuscript was made to look like some sort of elaborate enigma and that there is no intrinsic meaning behind it? Is it really just a bunch of gibberish? In other words, is it all just one big elaborate hoax?

In many ways, it would be easy to say that it is all a hoax. One could then believe that the reason the book does not make much sense is because it was never meant to. The real trouble with the hoax theory, though, is why. Who would go to such elaborate lengths to reap the benefit of an attention-getting hoax when the creators themselves would be long gone by the time the hoax became famous? After all, the book was largely unknown to most of the outside world until Wilfrid Voynich found it in 1912. Really, the only way that the hoax theory would work would be if Wilfrid Voynich himself was the creator.

This theory makes some sense since it became famous in his lifetime. In many ways, the sensational life of Wilfrid Voynich and his penchant for attention-getting sensationalism fits right in with that narrative. However, radiocarbon dating has ruled out Wilfrid Voynich as being the author of the manuscript. The pages, the ink (the ink was later tested at the University of Chicago and found to date back hundreds of years), and everything else about the manuscript is far too old to have been Wilfrid Voynich's creation.[i]

However, that is not to say that Wilfrid Voynich did not try to embellish some aspects of the manuscript and even the manner in which he found it. He also tried to hawk it and sell it in a tabloid-esque manner, but it seems pretty certain that Wilfrid Voynich was not the author of this confusion. The person behind the hoax—if there even is one—would have had to have been some strange soul from hundreds of years ago who never truly reaped the reward of his efforts.

So that, of course, brings us back to that same question—why? Why would some scribe from the Middle Ages make such an elaborate hoax? What would be the point?

The elaborate contents of the manuscript seem to indicate something meaningful (even if strange) in its intent. Then again, there are some who have argued that this is the true genius of the manuscript. The Voynich Manuscript is indeed made up of gibberish, but it was made in such a way that it seems to have a deeper meaning than it actually does.

For what it is worth, this manuscript has driven many researchers and cryptographers a bit mad. They find clues that seem to take them tantalizingly close to cracking some sort of hidden code, only to realize in the end that it is just as incomprehensible as ever. It is a mystery that may never be solved.

---

[i] Kennedy, Gerry. *The Voynich Manuscript: The Mysterious Code That Has Defied Interpretation for Centuries.* 2006. Pg. 26.

If you enjoyed this book, a review on Amazon would be greatly appreciated because it would mean a lot to hear from you.

To leave a review:
1. Open your camera app.
2. Point your mobile device at the QR code.
3. The review page will appear in your web browser.

Thanks for your support!

Here's another book by Captivating History that you might like

OPERATION MINCEMEAT

A CAPTIVATING GUIDE TO THE DARING DECEPTION THAT CHANGED THE COURSE OF WORLD WAR II

CAPTIVATING HISTORY

Free Bonus from Captivating History (Available for a Limited time)

Hi History Lovers!

Now you have a chance to join our exclusive history list so you can get your first history ebook for free as well as discounts and a potential to get more history books for free!

Simply visit the link below to join.

Or, Scan the QR code!

captivatinghistory.com/ebook

Also, make sure to follow us on Facebook, X, and YouTube by searching for Captivating History.

Further Reading and References

Belfield, Richard. *The Six Unsolved Ciphers: Inside the Mysterious Codes That Have Confounded the World's Greatest Cryptographers.* 2007.

Edwards, H. Robert. *Voynich Reconsidered: The Most Mysterious Manuscript in the World.* 2024.

Kennedy, Gerry. *The Booles and the Hintons: Two Dynasties that Helped Shape the Modern World.* 2017.

Kennedy, Gerry. *The Voynich Manuscript: The Mysterious Code That Has Defied Interpretation for Centuries.* 2006.

Levitov, Leo. *Solution of the Voynich Manuscript: A Liturgical Manual for the Endura Rite of the Cathari Heresy, The Cult of Isis.* 1987.

Voynich, Wilfrid. *A Preliminary Sketch of the History of the Roger Bacon Manuscript.* 1921.

Image Sources

[1] https://commons.wikimedia.org/wiki/File:Voynich_Manuscript_(66).jpg
[2] https://commons.wikimedia.org/wiki/File:Voynich_Manuscript_(3).jpg
[3] https://commons.wikimedia.org/wiki/File:Wilfrid_Voynich_c1920.jpg
[4] https://commons.wikimedia.org/wiki/File:Voynich_Manuscript_(32).jpg
[5] https://commons.wikimedia.org/wiki/File:Voynich_manuscript_bathtub2_example_78r_cropped.jpg

Made in United States
Troutdale, OR
09/11/2025